Cameron's Smile

Raising a deafblind child

Special thanks to Megan Paul – Editor and Friend.

Thank you to all those who have supported our journey

and helped my dreams become a reality.

"My little boy has never seen a smile but knows

exactly how to make one when he is happy".

Diagnosis

I dreamt of a healthy baby boy. I mean that is what everybody wishes for, right? As long as they are healthy, that is all that matters. But what happens when those dreams are snatched away? I was stricken with grief for a child I held in my arms and there was nobody I could talk to about those feelings – nobody who could even begin to comprehend what we were going through.

This tiny baby was placed on my chest within seconds of being born - I was in a bubble of love, where nothing else mattered. He had light golden skin, with dark brown hair, with the most perfect little pout. Cameron. A name for the most beautiful little boy.

'Welcome to the world,' I whispered. 'I can't wait to introduce you to your big sister Morgan'.

Little did I know our bubble was soon to burst and there was nothing I could do to change that.

The first few weeks were hard, my baby would sleep all day and wake all night. I had been here before with my daughter, and I knew it was just another stage we had to get through. Everybody who visited joked about how he was always sleeping and that they were never able to catch a glimpse of his eyes. Why wouldn't my baby open them? Then one day as the sunlight shone through the patio doors, he opened his eyes, and the rays created a golden haze across his face. But that's when I saw it: a tiny yellow dot on his left pupil. Is this the reason he has been so reluctant before? Google sent me on a downward spiral of cancerous tumours and blindness. The pit of my stomach began to ache. I had never noticed the dot before and surely the hospital doctors would have picked it up if there was a problem with my baby's eyes.

I couldn't wait for his newborn check up. Something had to be done straight away and within hours we were sat in a clinic room of our local surgery. I told the GP our concerns as she struggled to examine his tightly scrunched up eyes.

'He has never attempted to look towards the little toys I wave around in his face,' I told her. 'It's like he looks straight through me'.

The natural mother instinct in me knew something was different about him, but every ounce of my body was praying I had it terribly wrong.

An emergency referral was sent to our local eye hospital, and we were sent home to wait for a phone call. How could I just go home, sit around doing nothing, whilst all these fears were flying around my head? My head sunk

into Adam's shoulders as the tears began to flow. Things

like this don't happen to people like us. This nightmare

needs to end.

Waiting for our referral was torture. Every second of

everyday, sat waiting, staring at the phone hoping it would

light up - nobody was acting fast enough, and it sent me

into a rage. My head was spinning, yet I still had to wake

up every 4 hours throughout the night, exhausted, to feed

a baby who just needed his mummy. But his feeds began

to come back up each time, until we reached a stage

nothing was being held down. Enough is enough, there is

something seriously wrong, is it connected or just a

strange coincidence? What ever is happening, he needs

to be seen by the hospital and he needs to be seen

straight away.

9

The doctors were sure it was gastroenteritis and after a few days we would be able to go back home and enjoy our baby. Then the doctor began to shine a light in his little eyes that were now beginning to open more and more. Something unrelated was going on here. Suddenly we were in-patients and the referral we were longing for was pushed through.

'Cataracts' the doctor suggested, 'usually present in premature babies'.

But my baby was full term, and he passed all the newborn checks. What was going on? None of this made sense. Words were being thrown around that I had never even heard before.

We were transferred to the eye hospital, just minutes away

from the local children's hospital we were staying in. We

sat in an overflowing waiting room, longing for answers. I

just wanted the ground to swallow me up as people smiled

and cooed at my newborn on their way past. The clinician

called our family name, and we entered a large room with

just a sink and an empty grey hospital couch. There was

an overpowering smell of antiseptic, something that would

soon become an ever-familiar aroma. The nurses took my

little boy out of my arms and began to swaddle him in the

warm blue cotton hospital blankets. They slowly placed

eye drops into each eye to act as an anaesthetic whilst

they examined more closely. They placed what I can only

describe as a large clamp in front of his head to hold his

eyes wide open. I was mortified and stepped outside the

room, not wanting to watch a second longer. Adam came

out and squeezed my hand as my eyes welled up. I felt

11

physically sick. I lent back against the wall that separated us from the nurses, as I listened to the shrill cries of my fragile little boy.

We were seated in the consultants' office, and I released a huge sigh of relief as my baby was placed in my arms once more. I wished I could be stronger for him, he needed me to be there for him, I should never have left that room. That was the first time I heard the words 'Norrie Disease'. We were handed a leaflet and before we knew it our baby was whisked into theatre, preparing for a general anaesthetic to undergo an MRI scan of his brain.

How could someone so tiny go through so much within weeks of entering this world? I could not hold back the immense pain riffling through my body as he became limp in his Daddy's arms. And that was it. We were asked to exit the room to leave him with complete strangers. It felt

so wrong not being able to stay and hold onto his tiny little

fingers. The crescendo of the ticking clock echoed through

the empty corridors as we waited for what seemed like

hours.

The MRI confirmed our worst fears. Norrie Disease, a rare

genetic condition that mainly affects males, causing

complete blindness and a secondary symptom of

progressive hearing loss. He was being referred for

genetic testing. My little boy was never going to see my

face, let alone his own reflection. Ever. Of course, he

wasn't going to lose his hearing too, I just wouldn't let that

happen. Out of all the cards we have been dealt, living in

total darkness just felt like life was over before it had even

begun. Surely it couldn't get much worse. He couldn't

develop the possible additional symptoms this cruel

13

disease brings. This was too much information to process. This must be a mistake. He would have to receive treatment so we could have the little boy we longed for back home again, I told myself. All this will be a distant memory, I was sure of it. But there was no treatment, no magic cure. We were sent home to begin our new lives with a blind baby. This is not the way things were meant to be.

Each time I relayed the news to family members and friends, I had to relive those painful moments over and over. I didn't want it to be true. I didn't want to say the words out loud. I didn't want the sympathy and pity – it stung. I wanted to shut the world out and disappear. I was numb, an empty feeling I have never experienced before. And I wouldn't wish it on my worst enemy.

I needed solid support to hold me up whilst my world was crumbling beneath my feet, but it seemed it was Adam and I against the world. The people I needed the most couldn't create the security blanket I desperately needed. And it was then I realised who was truly there in the darkest time of my life. What was our future going to look like? I couldn't see happiness in it. I couldn't see anything at all. The future didn't even bare thinking about.

Despite sobbing into my pillow each night, I managed to somehow find the strength to wake up each day. I would take a long hard sniff as I held my son's soft newborn skin against my face. There was something so comforting about the fresh talc smell of a tiny human I once cradled in my belly. I felt an overwhelming amount of love run through my veins, something I never knew I would be capable of again after my first born. I watched as his big

15

sister sang lullabies and his Daddy rocked him to sleep in his tiny wicker basket. Something so beautiful, yet so painful at the same time.

The time soon came for geneticists to take blood samples from Cameron and me. There were still so many unanswered questions as to why this had happened to our family. Were we ever going to see answers? I relived every minute of my pregnancy with no explanations. I mapped a family tree – but still no clues. Going over and over the same process, but no further forward. We then had to wait twelve weeks for results. What would that even look like and what could we do with that information?

The day came where my mobile phone flashed to an unknown number. I held my breath as I picked up the call.

'Cameron's blood results confirm a mutation on the NDP gene'.

A mutation. That word made me feel like something was horrifically wrong with my child, despite how beautiful and perfect he looked to me.

'Your blood results show the exact same mutation as Cameron's results, meaning you hold a carrier status of Norrie Disease'.

Those two hideous words I never wanted to hear again. My knees went weak, and I stumbled back onto the unmade bed. This was all my fault. Something inside me made my little boy turn blind and I somehow had to live with knowing he had a disease I gave him. The guilt ate me up inside. I felt ashamed. Not fit to be a mother. How could I tell Adam what I had given his son? He would despise me even more than I despise myself.

Of course, that was so far from the truth. Something sent to destroy our world brought us closer together. We felt solid and unbreakable. We were both sharing the most unimaginable pain that no one else could understand. We had each other and we had to stay strong for our two little children who needed us for absolutely everything. At a time when we could easily have been torn apart, we anchored down and promised to make it through.

I found comfort in the internet. I would spend hours researching online, getting lost in forums and medical documents containing jargon. I needed to inform myself of everything there is to know about this rare condition that most doctors had never even heard of. I needed to know what it could bring, what life could look like, and what

impact it would have on my son's future. I needed to

connect with others who were experiencing the same. I

needed hope. I needed to cling to something.

I stumbled across an online support group where patients

from around the world were living with Norrie. This was my

safe haven that held a key to a door I was desperately

trying to open. I was scared to enter, but I needed to gain

knowledge on this unexpected chapter of our lives.

Suddenly things didn't seem so lonely anymore. I was

speaking to people who were oceans apart, yet who never

felt so close. There were adults who had lived a full and

happy life and could give me their first-hand experiences

of the way they perceive the world.

I often wondered how my blind child would smile. He had

never seen how to shape his mouth or mimic others facial expressions. I wondered how he would learn and reach all the typical milestones his older sister had. I wondered if he knew who I even was and how our bond would possibly develop.

.

But I remember that first smile more than any other moment in my life. The first giggle. The first sign of happiness. A simple tickly kiss on his naked belly. Repeated over and over again, as happy tears streamed down my face. Something ignited inside me, and I felt like I could see clearly for the first time in months. My son had never saw a smile but knew exactly how to make one. That is all that really mattered to me. My heart was full, and the dark clouds began to roll away.

My little man brought me so much happiness, but it was

still too painful to be around others. Cousins being born within days of each other, and all the baby groups and classes we should be enjoying. I couldn't stop comparing and it hurt my heart - it was the thief of joy. I watched as these babies looked towards their toys and engaged in play, whilst my child could barely use his neck muscles to lift his head up. A jealous rage built deep in the pit of my stomach and although I would never voice it, I hated my baby being different.

I needed to be around others who just got it and reached out to a local group. That first visit changed my whole perspective. I dragged Adam along, as I was too nervous to enter alone. Although I didn't have the confidence to speak in front of others, I wanted to listen. The room was full of parents who had been on this journey much longer than we had and all their children still had some useful

21

vision. Again, I couldn't help but compare. I sat back in my chair and listened as they spoke about their sadness, things that I just longed for, but they took for granted. I didn't feel like I belonged. An outcast wherever I went. We left the room and I turned to Adam.

'I never want to be that parent' I cried. 'The one who moans about such trivial things, complaining my child is a burden'.

It was time to start living, albeit a new way of living. Now it was about more than just surviving.

Those parents who sat in that room, of course their feelings were valid. I felt the pain they spoke of, but I didn't want to still be experiencing that same pain years later. It couldn't always be about what my child could not do. How could he ever be happy if he were surrounded by despair? It was time to flip the narrative and focus on the positives.

Looking back at that first year, I now reflect on how much we overcame. At the time, there wasn't a chance to catch our breath. Cameron was put under general anaesthetic numerous times for evaluations and to be treated for Glaucoma amongst other things. His eyes needed to be as comfortable and pain free as possible but watching him go to theatre never got easier. When I had to leave him a part of my heart left my body and would only return once he was back in my arms. I would wake in the night to the strange aroma of antiseptic and relive each moment spent inside those hospital walls. All the nurses knew our names and it began to feel like a second home. This was not where I wanted to call home.

Over the next few years, just as we got back up on our feet, life would throw us a curveball and we would come crashing back down again. I didn't understand why we deserved this. I have made mistakes in my past and haven't always been the person I would have liked to be, but I never did anything to justify this amount of tough luck as diagnosis after diagnosis were added to Cameron's huge medical file. He was nonverbal, autistic and soon needed gastrostomy surgery, but none of those things stung like the words Norrie Disease. When was it going to change?

Hearing loss

I said that my little boy was not going to develop the secondary symptoms of this disease. Every ounce of my soul truly believed that. I was not going to stand back and let my blind baby be robbed of yet another vital sense. He couldn't slip into a world of silent darkness; I was not going to allow that.

Research led me to believe that if he were going to experience those symptoms, it would be in his early twenties. That seemed so far away, something that I didn't even have to think about just yet.

Each year he would be monitored by audiology, but my heart told me his hearing was safe and the chances of that deteriorating was slim.

But it did. It happened to us. It happened to my little boy much sooner than anticipated. My happy, bubbly, fun, music-loving little boy. He was just three precious years old. One day he had full hearing and the next it was completely gone in one ear – just like that. It felt like a sick joke; I had just about got to grips with my child's blindness.

We started to see there was so much more to life than just vision. I would close my eyes and feel the vibrating beat of the music he would joyfully kick his legs along to. I watched as he listened intently to the hustle and bustle of the world around him. He got so much happiness from the little things I had never really noticed before, because I was previously too busy looking rather than experiencing the world through my other senses.

With the rapid deterioration in his hearing, it seemed certain that his happiness would be ripped away all over again, just like at the very beginning of this journey.

I was right back at that mourning period all over again, grieving for my son's hearing. If I was feeling this way, how must he be coping? His behaviour was that of a little boy so scared of his world changing. He had to adapt to hearing loss in a world he already could not see. I couldn't see how this was going to work. How unfair it seemed for him to be blind and deaf. I didn't want him to be either of the two, but surely one sensory loss was enough.

I needed to hold his hand and never let go, he was never going to be alone.

The audiologist came and sat next to the hospital bed as

Cameron began to stir from the anaesthetic.

'No response from the right ear.'

Those are all the words I can recall.

'What about a hearing aid'? I asked.

Surely this could be fixed, and we could go home to enjoy

all those tiny things once more.

'Sorry,' the audiologist whispered before handing me the

report.

How could his hearing be there one day and gone the

next? There were no warning signs. I wasn't prepared for

this in spite of his diagnosis. He was too young to be

developing these symptoms. It was too late for an aid in

that side. He had to solely rely on his left ear that

thankfully still had full hearing.

Once again, we were discharged to a different life with what felt like a different child.

He needed to guide my way because I was honestly so lost.

I felt like I had failed him all over again. The pain in my heart was far more intense than when we very first received his diagnosis of Norrie. Now I wasn't just grieving for his blindness - it was a double whammy. He was now going deaf despite how adamant I was that he would never suffer. But was he suffering? His smile still remained, and it gave me the hope I needed.

All of a sudden, we were thrust into a world of hearing loss, where we would meet new professionals and begin to adapt the world around him. Yet no one could understand the emptiness I had inside. There was no one I could turn to apart from Adam. And again - it was just the two of us against the world. He was the only one who knew my heartache and could see my heart bleed behind closed doors. I never knew one family could feel so much tormented agony. This life was so isolating.

As I watched my little boy pull the Bluetooth speaker towards his left ear, I watched his face light up as his favourite drum and bass music played. I sat back in awe as I witnessed him adapting to the hand he had been dealt. He still found a way to get so much out of life, and it seemed nothing was ever going to hold him back. If he could cope with this, it was my reason to remain strong.

I had seen that magical smile so many times before, the one where his whole face beams and its beauty takes my breath away. I have never seen that in anybody else before, it was unique and so precious.

This happiness too was short lived and just a few years later I began to watch Cameron's behaviour change. He was scared again, and I could see his world was changing once more. Each night he would grip my arm tightly whilst fighting against his tiredness, refusing to fall asleep. I would hold his head against my chest as he cried out in distress. He would angrily thump his head with his fists, as I used all my strength to prevent him. He was so strong; I couldn't stop it.

Back and forth we went to the doctor's surgery and

hospitals. The tainted smell of antiseptic sent him into a rage. He hated this place where he had previously experienced so many bad things. Traumatised by so many needles and I.Vs over the years, he wasn't going to cooperate.

I begged for professionals to listen. My child had to face so many challenges, but each day he would wake up with the most beautiful smile and appreciation for life.

I knew something was drastically wrong this time. My nonverbal little boy was communicating through his behaviour that he needed us to help him. Why wasn't anyone helping?

Morphine and tramadol are types of pain relief no child

should require. His behaviour was telling us something was clearly going on and we needed to act. This was just the beginning of a lifelong battle, fighting against professionals, begging for them to listen. It shouldn't have to be this hard, I thought. They should want to help take away his pain, no matter how hard it was to uncover.

After what seemed like weeks of hell, struggling to sleep, and watching my happy child slip away from me, a general anaesthetic was finally arranged to investigate further. So far, all the observations had come back normal, but this behaviour was far from it. That motherly instinct had kicked back in, and I was frantically begging to be heard. It needed to be an easy answer, some sort of infection that could be treated, so we could get back to the life we had created.

Once again, the heartache tore through my body. The consultant returned before my baby had even left the theatre.

A chronic infection was found in his already deaf ear, but there was more.

His hearing in his left ear wasn't as responsive as before. He now had a moderate hearing loss in that side. How was this happening all over again? When would I wake from this nightmare?

So much anger spilled from within. I knew something had been terrorising him for weeks, yet it had taken every ounce of energy to get our voices heard. I wanted to be proved wrong. I needed it to be a quick fix. There needed to be an end to all this torment. The truth was that this darkness would always be lurking in the corners of our lives, waiting to jump out and attack its prey. That prey was my child. My darling precious boy.

Here we were again, sitting in yet another overflowing waiting room.

Another hospital, and yet another new consultant. Sometimes I wondered how we fitted in living life when there were so many medical appointments to attend. It was a hot August, the kids were all home from school for the summer and we should have been sitting outside in the sunshine somewhere, not within these four walls yet again.

My heart was pounding as I wondered what lay ahead. I

squeezed Cameron's hand as he sat beside me in his wheelchair.

'You're going to be a brave boy today, whilst we try out something new.'

I lent in towards his left ear as I tried to prepare him. I wasn't sure how much he could understand, but I always made sure I spoke to him about everything around us.

The audiologist lent across and pushed an aid into his left ear. I held my breath and clutched my phone, ready to turn the camera on. I had started to capture as much as I could over the years because these little snippets meant so much. So many people sat in that room that day, waiting and watching as we prayed for a response. And there it was: the most stunning smile spread across his perfect little lips as he listened through his new hearing aid to the sound of the tambourine.

A sense of euphoria filled the room and I felt like my heart was about to burst. To see my little boy gain something so precious back was certainly a memory that will always be etched in my mind.

I would never take a moment for granted again. I would savour this moment and hold onto it forever.

I do not know when or if more hearing loss will occur, so for now we will live every day just like it's our last.

Looking to the future, he will one day be a candidate for cochlear implants, and although this isn't the journey I hoped for, I thank my lucky stars for the technology we

have out there.

Siblings

Raising my first-born daughter Morgan was a world away from the life we lived with Cameron. Giving birth at just 19 years old, I was thrown into the world of motherhood, and I did it to the best of my abilities.

With white, blonde hair and beautiful blue eyes, this little girl looked up to me as her role model. Looking back, I think about how selfish I was at times - maybe I wasn't quite ready to be a Mum. I tried my best and that was all that I could offer her. She was an only child, and I could at least give her all my time.

She was a confident child with a pinch of sass. She would make us laugh with her silly dance moves, singing along to the music channel with my hairbrush in her hand. She didn't have a care in the world.

The day I announced I was carrying her brother, she cried. Of course, she wanted a baby sister and I had to send him back. He wasn't allowed here, she refused. When Adam brought her to visit on the day, I lay in the hospital bed cradling her brother who was just hours old, she ran straight over with pride written all over her face.

'Cameron, I love him,' she whispered.

She was happy with a brother after all.

How could I explain to a 4-year-old about something I struggled to wrap my head around? We needed to be honest, but I didn't want her to be scared.

We sat her down within days of his diagnosis and told her all about Cameron's eyes being underdeveloped and him being unable to see. She asked me many questions about things like how he would ever walk, some questions I didn't know the answers to, but we owed it to her to be as honest as possible.

I couldn't have wished for a better sister to Cameron. She was caring, kind and compassionate, and their bond was just something else. I watched their remarkable relationship flourish as she cared for her brother in a way, I never knew possible. She would often sing him lullabies and make him giggle in a way nobody else could. I saw this fire in her belly, just like her mumma's, and I just knew she was going to protect him.

It wasn't all sunshine and rainbows, though. Life was hard, but it was going to be even tougher for her - as a sibling to a disabled child. I missed her terribly with every hospital admission. I could see that she worried immensely for her baby brother, and she carried a weight on her shoulders no child her age should bare. Adam and I tried to take the strain, but she was always going to worry about someone she loved so dearly. She never stopped making me proud.

During her primary school years, she was determined to raise awareness. She spoke about her brother with triumph, so of course she jumped at the chance to hold a day in school to teach her classmates all about the impact of deaf blindness. They all joined in as they finger spelt their names, using the deafblind manual alphabet on their hands. She came home to show us over and over again, talking about it for days.

She had to sacrifice so much at such a young age. There

44

was once a time she had me all to herself, and now she had to share me with a baby who needed me in such a different way. I worried endlessly she was going to resent me or her brother. I was scared she would build up a hatred for all that she witnessed - but I don't think that could have been further from the truth.

There were so many times I had let her down, I just couldn't always split myself in two, and a lot of the time she had to miss out on doing things she loved. I felt so guilty trying to juggle both of their needs.

No matter what I did, I never thought I would be able to get it right, and I was so conscious of that.

I hated the thought of her being neglected or forgotten.

Some nights all I wanted to do was crash my weary head on the pillow, but I know I needed to manage my time so she could get just a small snippet of what she deserved.

After finding out Cameron's diagnosis, Adam and I made the decision to not go on to have anymore children. I still felt an incredible guilt inside, knowing I was responsible for this gene. I couldn't handle the heartache of going through something similar all over again, and I felt it was just unfair on Morgan and Cameron to bring another baby into this family when I felt everyday was already a struggle to give them both my all.

We took all the precautions and having another baby was never at the forefront of our minds.

At the time when we were trying to overcome another hurdle, adapting to the world of hearing loss, I was stricken with a grief that made me physically sick. Unbeknown to me, what I was experiencing was in fact morning sickness.

Those two little blue lines appeared in front of me, something so many people can only wish for. Yet here I was panic stricken instead of ready to celebrate. This wasn't part of the plan. I was so scared.

Adam was over the moon. Secretly I knew he wanted more children, but the truth was it was never going to be easy. I made the phone call to the geneticist.

I couldn't tell a soul until we knew what to expect.

It was so hard to hide the sickness or even make it through the days, whilst continuing to care for a blind child and his sister.

I was 9 weeks along when the doctors took a blood sample, such a basic test that would provide life changing answers. The test would determine the baby's gender and if they would be affected by the same gene as Cameron's. We had to wait two long painful weeks for those results. This felt like my life now: continuously waiting for bad luck to rear its ugly head.

Again, my phone flashed to an unknown number. How many times had I been here before?
'It's a girl,' said the consultant.

At just 11 weeks pregnant I found out I was carrying a precious girl inside me.

I never knew I could find out this information so early. 'She will be unaffected, as Cameron's condition is only usually found in males'.

Tears streamed down my face. Was this happy tears, or tears of guilt? I had so many conflicting emotions, I was confused.

A huge weight had lifted from my shoulders, yet I still felt so much pain. I felt blessed to be carrying a healthy baby girl, but an immense feeling of sadness for the what ifs. What if it had been a boy? There would have been a 50% chance of him having Norrie Disease. How would we have coped with that? I often questioned myself and would slowly slip into a world of self pity if I continued to do so.

It was time to embrace the world of whatever will be, will be. It was time to acknowledge what was happening instead of focusing on the what could have been.
I had been here before; I knew I was strong enough. I knew I would love my children unconditionally, no matter what circumstances came our way. There would always be those thoughts that I desperately tried to lock away in the back of my mind.

I knew what I was about to face as I announced our news. Judgement. People who hadn't walked a mile in our shoes.

'How will you cope with a new born?'

'Oh, you're going to have *three* children now'.

The snide comments hit me deeply because of course I had these worries myself. How was I going to meet Cameron's needs whilst caring for a vulnerable tiny human being alongside the sass of a 7-year-old?

This was it, I reminded myself. This was our family. Who cared what others thought? I was going to do this.

The day my beautiful 'Indie' was born, I broke down in tears. Everything that had built up inside me came spilling out. She had the same blue eyes as her brother and sister with dark brown hair and the perfect pout I had seen in Cameron. She was chubby and her little rolls filled every part of her baby grow. After the toughest pregnancy, I felt so much relief that she was finally here. Despite the genetic testing, I had so many fears. I almost felt paranoid, and I couldn't enjoy her as I was meant to. Everyday I would examine her eyes, looking for signs. I would wave brightly coloured toys in her face, comparing her to her older siblings. Every day I was holding my breath waiting for something to happen.

But it didn't. It wasn't until she was around three months old that those feelings started to slowly roll away. I was wasting precious time worrying about things way out of my control.

Indie is unaffected by Norrie Disease, but both girls still have a 50% chance of carrying the gene mutation

Cameron and I have. This is going to impact their lives and the guilt of that will never ever go away.

Despite those challenges, my family is now complete. Three siblings to build a beautiful bond with one another. Their lives look different from most of their peers, but different doesn't have to be negative.

I still have those same feelings I felt with my first-born Morgan. The constant worry: am I giving both girls enough of my time and attention? A mother's guilt never eases despite the hand we had been dealt. I would never allow them to take on the caring role, but the impact of having a disabled brother still means they are recognised as young carers. Life can be challenging for them; they have had to grow beyond their years, but they have developed the most beautiful souls.

They understand differences in the world and embrace it. They are passionate, kind and caring. They have a gentle nature and will always advocate for what they believe in, and I'm so glad they have got each other.

Indies relationship with Cameron didn't come easy at first, she had to be old enough to initiate those first interactions with her older brother. But before long she was guiding his hands and eager to learn how to interact with him.

It really was such a magical thing, sitting back and watching their sibling bond grow.

There are still hard days, easy days and all the days in

between, but I wouldn't change my family for the world. I'm

so happy all those things I never planned for happened

anyway. I am blessed.

Comparison

The thief of joy, yet I couldn't help myself. Wherever I go, whatever I do, I can't stop myself comparing our child to what would have been.

Nobody plans for a disabled child. Nobody wishes challenges and struggles on their loved ones. Yet here we were, faced with the unimaginable. These feelings should be spoken about and normalised. We are not bad people for having these feelings, it's human nature. Just don't unpack and live there.

Life is certainly an emotional rollercoaster. I faced grief at the very beginning, but I soon welcomed the breath-taking views I came across on the journey.

That doesn't mean to say there won't be rough days.

My mental health is constantly yo-yoing between the bad and the good, but my tour guide always provides the helping hand that I need. Cameron is the reason I remain so strong.

From an early age we immersed ourselves in groups for children just like him. I still compared, no matter how hard I tried not to. I felt lonely. It was extremely hard to come across another child who was completely blind or experienced the world just like Cameron.

Every time we left the house, he would cry. He found comfort in his home surroundings. New places were. frightening and the world wasn't equipped for a blind. child.

I remember asking myself, 'when will he walk'?

He never even crawled. It stung to know he was unable to do things like others of a similar age.

I had this checklist of typical milestones, and no one could prepare me for when things went off the plan. Now I know that there is no checklist or chart for a child. I felt like an outcast from the world, and I wish there were a way to change that for other parents.

We would attend groups for visually impaired children, but still found ourselves not being able to do the things others with limited sight could experience. I feel sick admitting that I was jealous. Despite their own struggles, I still envied the little sight they had and how I wish my son could have just a tiny glimpse, and what impact that would have on his life.

It's not something I can express freely: being jealous of others' disabilities. This is the raw reality of grief and comparison. I was always comparing and wishing my child had a little less to deal with. Those feelings often got buried deep down inside my soul. They could not be allowed at the forefront of my mind for long, because they would destroy any light that I saw before me.

It may take a while, but acceptance does come. I learnt that the sooner I could accept, the sooner I got to go out there and enjoy the life we were given.

I can't recall the exact moment I learnt to accept Cameron's diagnosis. It may not have been a specific day, but something that slowly developed with time. The more I played with him, loved him, and enjoyed him for who he was, the more manageable life became.

I remember his first steps at the age of three. He wobbled as he reached out for his Daddy. There was this sense of magic in the air and the celebration filled my heart.

Reaching milestones seems so much more special to me now. The tiny ones that we often take for granted warrant the hugest of festivities. My child will always find a way to experience the world in his own unique way. It doesn't have to look like how you or I do it.

Watching him learn to walk, I truly believed that was another hurdle crossed, but I wasn't prepared for the difficulties that came with it. Again, I couldn't help compare, even to his sisters. He still needed a wheelchair and was only able to tiptoe walk in familiar surroundings. I had to stop holding a picture of what things should look like. It was time to let go. Cameron would get there in his own time and in his own way. I just needed to be there to support him to blossom in his environment. I embrace him with love and celebrate him for all that he is.

The day he was diagnosed as autistic was the day, I felt a sense of relief. I could see it for all these years and I was desperate for others to understand him too. The way he experiences the world is a lot different to you or I. It's breathtaking to be able to understand that more clearly now and I just hope he can teach others, just like he taught me. I need to be a little less judgemental, more understanding. There is no comparison between the sun and the moon – they will shine when it's their time.

I often dreamt about hearing his voice for the first time. I looked at all the children around us developing speech and the skills to communicate. Every mother longs for the day their child says 'Mummy, I love you'. I needed to hear it.

I needed him to tell me how he was feeling and about all his wants and needs. That day still hasn't come. I struggled as he became frustrated trying to express himself. I felt stupid for not always understanding what he was trying to say. How much easier would it be if he could just tell me what was hurting, or that he was hungry or thirsty? It often felt like we were stuck at the newborn baby stage, trying to comfort him with food, cuddles or nappy changes. My child was much larger and stronger than a newborn baby and the challenges seemed far vaster.

I started to let go of what I imagined. Communication is far greater than just spoken word. I never really knew the true meaning behind that until my son showed me.

Cameron started using body language and gestures to make me aware of his needs and suddenly I just got it. I understood. Granted, I don't always understand or get it right at the beginning, but with patience and time he always shows me the way.

When he wraps his arms around me with a tight squeeze, pressing his nose against my cheek, with a husky little giggle, that is his way of telling me how much he loves me. I think there is far more power in that than any spoken word. He guides my hands and signs when he wants 'more' swinging, 'more' tickles or 'more' biscuits.

I watched in awe as he found his own way to express himself. That's when it hit me. It doesn't matter if he ever says a spoken word. There is a fierce amount of power in a nonverbal child who lets the world know exactly what they need. We must listen a little harder.

Sometimes I have to pinch myself and remind myself to stop comparing. Stop judging others. Step back and look at the bigger picture. There's so much more here to see. Comparison is the thief of joy. Start living your life, it's just as worthy as others.

Carer

Some people dislike this term, but the truth is, this is what I am. I am far more than the mum I planned to be. I am a mum, a carer, a therapist, an advocate, and all the things in between.

This isn't what I pictured my life to look like. I planned to return to work once my children hit school age. I wanted to map out a career and enjoy time that I needed to develop my own self worth. This was snatched away without warning.

The choice was taken away from me, something I took for granted before my life with Cameron. Even after my first born, I still managed to find childcare and go back to college to study. Yet life was different this time and I couldn't just leave my baby at a child minders. I suddenly had very limited choices and options when making decisions about my life.

I do not want to be pitied. Carers don't deserve to be looked at whilst others think 'I'm so glad that's not me'. We don't want the sorrow and the despair. Instead, we need support and that's why it is an important subject to be talked about.

Being a mum is hard work. Add being a carer on top of that and the load can often feel exhausting. It's not the caring for or loving my child that is the hard part. That comes so naturally and easily to me. It's the uphill battle against an unfair world that is far from accommodating. Nobody warned me or could even quite prepare me for this never-ending fight. Even if I had been told, I wouldn't have believed it.

It's true what they say: nobody can even begin to comprehend those battles until you are living this life yourself. I still can't get my head around the fact we live in a world that still hasn't caught up with what needs to be done to include disabled people.

It took eight years of suppressing feelings of exhaustion before it all became too much to bear. That was when I experienced my first panic attack. Nobody seems to talk much about those feelings. I felt a crushing feeling in my chest whilst gasping for air. I suddenly panicked at the thought of my son being in a world without his primary carer. It would leave me feeling so breathless I could barely lift my weak body out of bed.

Something needed to change, I needed more practical support, something I spent so long begging for.

Over the years something has changed within me. I wasn't the person I used to be before children and now I'm an even more different version of myself after caring for Cameron. Sometimes that is hard to accept. My character has completely changed. There are possibly many things I have missed out on over the years; at times I even feel like I may have lost myself a little. There is so much more that I have gained from life now and I am so thankful.

I was a selfish person growing up. I never truly acknowledged others' feelings and the impact of my actions, because I was the only one that mattered. I guess having children often changes that, but it didn't change for me until my eyes were opened to a completely different world.

I have always been shy and nervous in new situations and suddenly I was thrust into a world where I needed to be assertive. I needed to advocate for someone who didn't have a voice, and they needed me to have a fire in my belly that I didn't naturally have before. Maybe it had been silently there all along, waiting to be ignited. Before Cameron, I would be the one too nervous to join in, sitting on the side-lines, waiting, and wondering. In the last eight years I have been pushed so far out of my comfort zone that there is no going back to the person I once was.

I used to look at others and wish I had their confidence.

Over time I gained a new perspective and began to live the life I longed for. I needed to stop relying on others to hold my hand as I was being held back when they repeatedly let me down. It was time to stand up for my son's needs and make sure he got as much out of life as possible. That meant growing confidence that would allow the world to open up around us.

I am often questioned about how I find the resilience to cope.

'How do you just keep going, even in the dark times?' people want to know.

The truth is I do not have a choice. That choice was taken away from me at the very beginning. I mean, there are two options: to keep going or quit. What would happen if I quit? If Cameron can face challenges head on so fearlessly and bravely, I owe it to him to keep going, even on the days I struggle to find the strength.

When the most recent bout of anxiety left me exhausted, I had spent the past 8 years fighting a broken system. It was bound to get the better of me sooner or later.

Health and social care are designed to help families just like ours, yet there's an unrealistic criteria to be reached before they will provide the necessary support. Even then, the goal posts are continuously moved so far away that they feel almost unreachable. They count on us carers being so exhausted that we will just give up and keep quiet.

People don't always stick around when things get tough.

It's hard to make or even keep friends, and the family we

have aren't always the ones who share the same blood.

Relationships can be so different when caring for a child

with disabilities. It's so hard to maintain even the simplest

of things that we become unreliable. We don't always fit in,

yet we still desperately need that support system around

us.

I found myself begging for help with every hospital

admission. My son has profound and complex needs, yet

it's so hard to get the care he deserves. To constantly

seek support only to be let down time and time again is

demoralising. Why is my son's life less worthy than

others?

I had been fighting the same battle for years, ensuring my

kids got the same opportunities in life, but one day

the weight began to take its toll. The panic attacks took

over my whole body and came on thick and fast. I would

clutch my chest as I fell to the floor, scared of what was

happening. Breathing so fast and heavy, my heart felt like

it was pounding in the middle of my throat. The ambulance

crew turned up within minutes, and before I knew it, I was

hooked up to wires and monitors. I have witnessed so

many admissions over the years, but I wasn't used to

being the patient.

'Anxiety' the paramedics diagnosed.

I felt so embarrassed and ashamed.

'I am so sorry for wasting your time', I cried.

This wasn't a real emergency; I had never felt so silly.

They reassured me that it was real, and that it was serious. My anxiety and exhaustion had started to take its toll on my body physically and that's when I realised the importance of self care.

I am worthy of a support system for me and my family. If I am not fit and well, who will be there to care for my family? This is too much strain for Adam and I to carry whilst he juggles work and home life too.

Despite the pain I was experiencing, I summoned up the courage to spread awareness in the local media. My son and others just like him deserve more. The local authority finally agreed to put a care package in place, and we began to see a small glimpse of just the beginning of what he was entitled to, to allow him to live a rich and full life.

It takes a village to raise a child, but carers are often shut out of that village. We are standing on the outside looking in, banging on the soundproof glass that nobody can hear.

Exercise has certainly become my release. I need to be strong, not just physically but emotionally too. I struggle with anxiety, but I will not let it win.

Support often fell on professionals and paid carers who came into our home. They started off as complete strangers who saw my most private times behind closed doors. I wear my heart on my sleeve and I can't help but get attached to those who are a part of our journey, no matter how short the time span. I'm letting these people help look after the most precious jewel I have, something so vulnerable and fragile, that has only ever solely relied on me previously. It's a fine line to tread, the one where I need to let go and enable independence but still be there on call, probably for the rest of my life.

There is no doubt Cameron has changed me. I really believe he has shaped me into the person I always should have been. He has given me so many opportunities I would have never gained without him. My strength came from him. He taught me resilience and bravery. He taught me the true meaning of happiness. I hope I've made him proud. I am certainly proud of being a carer and the community I am now part of. There is something so powerful about that role. I am more than a Mum of three, I am a carer too – that is part of my identity now.

Cameron's smile

There is something so unique about that smile. I longed for it from the very first day I learnt of his diagnosis - and quite frankly it saved me from the depths of despair.

Everyone who has met him comments on his happiness and that beautiful smile. Some find it hard to believe that disabled people can face many challenges, but still live an incredibly happy life.

I was certainly naïve in thinking 'how could my son ever be happy, living in a world of darkness?' I feel so silly even letting those thoughts run through my mind. I have never come across anyone who shows so much appreciation for life and everything in it.

If people ask, of course I will tell them Cameron is blind. It is an important piece of information, so that they can be aware of how to interact with him.

'I'm so sorry', seems to be the common response.

Trust me, you will soon learn: there is absolutely nothing to be sorry about.

For a long time my baby would explore the world by lying on his back and reaching out his arms to feel within his grasp. He was so nervous to open up the palm of his hands and stretch out his little fingers. His hands were so sensitive, helping him to 'see' the world in his own special way. As soon as an unfamiliar texture or object brushed against his fingertips, his fists would clench, and he would almost pull away from the world. He was nervous. It must have been so confusing for him to gain an understanding of everything around him. With time and support, I witnessed his confidence grow. His hands would slowly unclench and he began to gain excitement and curiosity. I mean, that takes some bravery, to finally build up the courage to explore the unknown. It took many years, but he has since developed such a fearless nature, something I really admire and only wish I had more of.

Lying his back against a resonance board for the first time, I could already see his anticipation growing. A resonance board was something I hadn't come across before, but I soon learnt it was a simple, yet amazing piece of equipment for a blind child. It was a thin raised sheet of wood that provided tactile and auditory feedback. I placed a Bluetooth speaker on top of the board, next to Cameron's kicking legs. I scrolled through the playlist on my phone until I reached his Daddy's favourite drum and bass collection. The strong beat to the music would vibrate through the wood against his back and over every part of his body. He started to flap his arms and legs in excitement, and I could see the full sensory experience he was getting from just the sound of music playing. He would giggle and wriggle around as the vibrations tickled his back. I had never played with my baby in this way before, but I could see the joy he was getting from feeling every single beat, and that's where his love of music truly began.

Even as the years went by and his hearing began to deteriorate, there was still something so magical about watching him experience the sound of his favourite drum and bass music. It's so much more than just listening to a song. It dances through his whole body and the joy radiates from within.

Cameron's perception of the world is no doubt much different from yours and mine.

Visits to the beach fill him with elation. As he sits down in the fine golden sand, he runs his fingers through every grain. He scoops a handful, again and again, as it slowly sprinkles away on the wind. He strokes his bare feet over the desert-like ground, manipulating the grit between his toes. He raises his head, facing up to the sky, as the sun warms his face. He giggles at the sensation of the wind blowing against his ears. He stands up with the help of my guiding hand, and I support him to walk toward the shore. The wet squidgy sand pushes through the gaps of his toes as he gets closer to the ocean. The sea spray hits his face and takes him by surprise. He flaps his hands with excitement as he seeks more.

The experience is absolutely breathtaking, and so much more than you could ever envision. I'm so thankful for him opening up my world in this way.

Live life with no limits. This is the motto he has firmly instilled in us. I repeated this over and over in my head as I signed him up to the next adventure.

Parasailing is something many would be too frightened to consider. My little boy couldn't tell me if it was something he wanted to do so I had to make that judgement for him in the hope it was the right one. Was I making the right choice? He could cry and hate every moment, but I knew my baby better than anyone in this world and I had to trust my gut. He's got this thrill-seeking, adrenaline junkie character about him and needs to take the leap. His limited mobility and need for extra support to access activities shouldn't be a barrier to new experiences.

As we fitted the life jacket around his tiny waist, he knew something exciting was about to happen. We stepped onto the boat as it gently rocked against the wind. We headed out to sea and he laughed more and more as the boat thrashed against the waves. I held my breath as Cameron, Morgan and Adam were strapped into their harnesses. 'Hold onto him, Adam' I whispered, nervously sitting back to watch with Indie in my arms.

As they ascended into the air, I saw Cameron's hands

reach up to feel the wind and my daughter screamed with excitement. All their faces were a picture, as I grabbed my camera and set it to record.

'Wow' I thought. 'My deafblind little boy is doing it, he's having the time of his life, living life with no limitations.'

How freeing to be up there in the clouds, feeling the extreme force of the wind against your face whilst almost floating weightlessly in the sky. I will never forget that day, the day tears filled Adam's eyes as their feet touched the deck once more. He got to experience such a powerful moment with his children, and I knew how much it made him happy to see his son's face filled with delight.

I remember Cameron's first school sports day so vividly. He had not yet learnt how to walk and needed to be pushed in his wheelchair to go outdoors. Many of the games were adapted, and we supported him to take part, rolling balls down a ramp to score a strike and throwing bean bags in the hoops. Then came the obstacle course.

Instead of pushing a heavy chair, his Daddy scooped him up and started running, manoeuvring around the equipment. As Adam ducked and jumped, Cameron was thrown across his daddy's shoulder as he laughed so hard from the bumpy ride. This was the role model Cameron needed, making sure he experienced everything fully. As they reached the end of the course, Adam guided Cameron's hand to ring the bell and every body let out an almighty cheer. What a feeling. I was so proud.

As Cameron grew bigger, the world felt like it was getting

smaller. Places were more difficult to visit, but we never wanted that to hold him back. Visiting the most inaccessible attractions, I struggle to carry him on my hip. We drag his wheelchair backwards across rough terrain, and Adam even lifts Cam in his chair up and down the most challenging of places.

No matter how tiring and tricky things get - we do it for love.

We do it to see Cameron's smile light up his face and the sheer gratitude that runs through his veins. We will always try and find a way to include him in the world.

Sometimes things get tough, and days don't always go to plan. There can be tears and tribulations - we may have to go home early and rekindle hope for another day. There are times I break down with frustration and anger, wondering why somethings never run as smoothly as I imagined. I am always reminded the best things in life aren't easy. If we hadn't experienced the dark times, the good times wouldn't be so wholesome. I cherish the beautiful memories and hold onto them so dearly because I have lived through anguish and trauma.

At the beginning of this journey, I would never have imagined our life to look this way. Hindsight is a wonderful thing. It has brought so much appreciation.

Wow, I really am lucky. There was a time I thought I was down on that.

Everyday I am reminded to count my blessings.

The future

Here comes the scary part. The future. Everyday I am left wondering what tomorrow will bring. If I focus too much on what's to come, a downward spiral will take its hold, whilst I fall into oblivion.

Norrie Disease has brought so many developing symptoms that tomorrow's plans are often out of my control. This scares me immensely. Control is something I desperately need. A storm cloud, known as progressive hearing loss, looms over our heads, and everyday it feels like it creeps closer.

There are days where I can sink into deep depression, thinking about things that are so far out of my reach. The worry makes me physically sick, as anxiety grasps its hold around my chest and begins to squeeze against my ribs.

Those early days were full of worries, as I desperately scrambled around in my own mind, trying to figure out what our life would look like. I would sob into my pillow each night, praying to wake from this nightmare. I was so frightened of the unknown path we were about to take. The future looked pretty bleak and desolate. As we began to live, the worrying future was still at the forefront of my mind.

My gorgeous little boy with his cheeky little ways. Will his quirkiness still be seen as cute and funny when he is a fully grown disabled man? Will society still accept him when his behaviours don't fit into the 'norm'? What about when we go out and visit all the places he loves? It only becomes more inaccessible and challenging as he grows.

Will I still be providing 24/7 care for my grown-up child, pad changing and feeding through a gastrostomy? So many questions for which I do not know the answers.

I remind myself not to spend too much time worrying about tomorrow as it only empties today of my strength. Instead, I have shifted my energy into what *can* be done. What *can* we do today to make it memorable? What *can* we do to make a change? There's a passion that burns fiercely inside me that will stand up and advocate for my precious boy's needs. I need to tell our story to others, so that I'm able to worry a little less about our future.

With awareness, understanding and acceptance, my little boy's road ahead looks more promising. I have been there so many times before, where somebody is hurt by inequality and exclusion.

Please know there are so many small things that can be done to make the world more inclusive.

Be the change people like my son so desperately need.

It is not his disability that holds him back, but the obscure world that continues to isolate him.

It often crosses my mind: what will happen when I am no longer here? Not many people would wish that their child go before them, but I can't imagine his existence without me here to provide his care. It scares me to my core. I am comforted to know he has his siblings who love him.

To look so far ahead destroys my inner soul. My thoughts cannot stay in that dark place for too long. What's to say that couldn't happen tomorrow, in a month or even a year from now?

There go my crazy thoughts again. I must reign them in.

Whilst it's sensible to plan ahead, somethings are so far out of my control - let's just live for the here and now. Live life to the full. Push yourself so far out of your comfort zone so that you never live a single day in regret.

I sometimes think about regretting those early days after diagnosis, maybe I could have done more. I ask myself: what is the point of regrets? All those thoughts, feelings, actions, and events have made me the person I am today.

They have shaped me into this human being that hopes for a better world where everybody lives side by side.

A stranger on the internet commented that disabled people like my son aren't worthy of life. That crushes my heart to even say those words out loud.

I need them to know he is more than worthy.

He's eight years old and has lived a much fuller life than most adults I know. He sees the world in such a beautiful way. If only more people had his innocence and purity, we would live in such a tranquil place. His smile has changed my life and I just know it's about to change the world too.

Printed in Great Britain
by Amazon

20055448R00058